HIDDEN GARDENS

OF BEACON HILL

FOURTH EDITION

Photographs by

PETER VANDERWARKER AND TOM LINGNER

THE BEACON HILL GARDEN CLUB, INC.
Boston, Massachusetts

The Hidden Gardens of Beacon Hill
Published in 1999 by the Beacon Hill Garden Club, Inc.
Box 302, Charles Street Station, Boston, Massachusetts 02114

Presidents:	Susan Birkett, 1996–1998
	Eugenie Walsh, 1998–2000

Editors:	Barbara W. Moore, Gail Weesner
Copy Editor:	Mary Frances Townsend
Designer:	Dede Cummings
Printing:	South China Printing Company Limited, Hong Kong

COVER:	Springtime in a garden on West Cedar Street
TITLE PAGE:	*Boy and Bird* by Bashka Paeff nestled in a Beacon Hill garden
BACK COVER:	Nineteenth-century figure of a goddess or maiden holding a scallop shell, with clematis

ACKNOWLEDGMENTS
The Editors gratefully acknowledge the advice and assistance of the following in the preparation of this edition: Charles Street Flowers, French Bouquet, Rouvalis Flowers, Inc., the Massachusetts Historical Society, and the members of the Beacon Hill Garden Club whose gardens appear on these pages.

Introduction and Dedication

In this closing year of the century, the Beacon Hill Garden Club turns seventy. As an introduction to this book, it seems appropriate to take a look backward to remember our founding members, the women and men who in 1929 saw potential in their drab laundry yards and made the first organized endeavor to change them into gardens. Those small early ventures took root and multiplied as more and more neighbors were prompted to make similar improvements. A modern overview of Beacon Hill reveals abundant greenery — the verdant legacy of our founders.

That same year several charter members opened their gardens to the public — a tradition that continues to the present day. The annual Hidden Gardens tour is a great neighborhood occasion, bringing out legions of volunteer workers and attracting thousands of visitors. Proceeds from this one-day event enable us to support an array of civic and neighborhood projects (see page 88).

A second backward glimpse will recall the year 1959, when a new generation of members developed the idea of publishing a small book of black-and-white photographs entitled *The Hidden Gardens of Beacon Hill*. That slim volume is now a collector's item, and along with the succeeding editions (1972 and 1986), it provides a valuable archive of the development of scores of city yards.

A guiding spirit behind the first three editions was Frances Minturn Howard (1905-1995), an accomplished poet and essayist and a member of this club for almost fifty years. We gratefully dedicate this Fourth Edition to her memory.

APRIL 1999

COLOR

The Garden of Mrs. Sarah T. Brewster
PINCKNEY STREET

The season begins with a display of bright spring bulbs rising from an established ground cover of English ivy. Yellow daffodils and a stone basket of orange tulips contribute dramatic color beneath an ancient horse chestnut. Planted a century ago, this handsome old tree dominates the garden and casts deep shadow throughout the summer. As the seasons progress, the ivy beneath the tree can be interplanted with shade-tolerant annuals — impatiens and begonias in summer, mums in the fall. A framed mural of a trompe l'oeil niche is surrounded by diamond-shaped trelliswork on the far wall.

ENCHANTMENT

The Garden of Mr. and Mrs. Amos Hostetter
LOUISBURG SQUARE

In this stylish terraced garden the area next to the house is formal, but below, enclosed by a low iron fence, is a miniature landscape, a Lilliputian woodland scene where a carpet of velvety moss creates a replica of the moist forest floor. All the plantings have white flowers: rhododendrons, azaleas, tulips, primroses, trillium, and three white redbuds, which bear their tiny blossoms on bare stems. A water baby astride a dolphin rises from a small pool while a life-sized stone cherub wearing a sundial stands to the left of the pool. This fairy-tale world is entered via a stepping-stone path that branches off to a white stone bench set against a backdrop of climbing hydrangea and ivy. This is a perfect gem of a garden, evoking the enchantment of a childhood dream.

CANOPY

The Garden of Mr. and Mrs. Richard Norton
OTIS PLACE

The fresh green foliage of a katsura tree rises above the sculptural bronze mound of a dwarf Japanese maple, while in the foreground pink dogwood blossoms mingle with the young spring leaves of a crabapple. By midsummer these four trees will weave together to create a summer canopy that shields the garden from the incessant traffic on Storrow Drive, just beyond the grape-stake fence. In fact the garden was rebuilt in 1958 in response to the construction of that highway, which necessitated a change in grade and an increased need for privacy. In the curved and tiered beds are tulips and the massed colors of several varieties of azalea, with overlapping flowering seasons for many weeks of consecutive bloom. In summer it becomes an all-green garden with evergreens and hostas rising from a ground cover of ivy.

ROMANCE

The Garden of Mr. and Mrs. Thomas H. Townsend
CHESTNUT STREET

A child bearing a scallop-shell birdbath sets the romantic tone for one of the
Hill's oldest gardens, which dates back some sixty years. Moreover, the house
is still occupied by the same family, who have saved the decorative features
of the old garden and replaced plants only when needed. The lead figure
stands above a small pool, and an Italian limestone putto is glimpsed behind
a flowering rhododendron. The hanging tassels of laburnum are light and
delicate against the tracery of Spanish wrought-iron gates, which separate
the upper garden from a lower level that can be used for parking. Nearby is
a brick wellhead equipped with a rope and pulley and oaken bucket —
constructed, it is said, atop a much older well that was discovered in this
yard in the 1930s. This garden has acquired character through the years, with
a timeless tranquillity and a sense of romance.

Hospitality

The Garden of Mrs. Charles J. Innes
PINCKNEY STREET

Glimpsed through a white latticed archway from a neighboring yard is one of the original Connecting Gardens — a group of courtyards that for many years were informally joined though privately owned and separately maintained. Though the ensemble is no longer complete, this scene captures the hospitable spirit of that old communal venture. The enormous charm of this fifty-year-old garden is its genial informality. In the words of its owner, it "has designed itself within its 'bones.' All the plants decide whether to be happy where they are." Recent years have seen the demise of several large ailanthus trees, so this is a sunnier garden than it once was. But it retains its old planting scheme of tough, mostly evergreen plants, reducing maintenance to a minimum. The large white azalea inside the gate began as a small Mother's Day plant, purchased at a local supermarket some twenty-five years ago.

RHYTHM

Two long, narrow gardens enlivened by serpentine lines

The Garden of Mrs. Jeanne Muller Ryan
CHESTNUT STREET

This elegant town garden has been created from a sunless passageway that once led to the service entrance of an 1820s Federal mansion. The current owner has made the space both intimate and interesting with several illusionary devices. The meandering walkway detracts from the verticality of the brick walls. Moreover, the end of the courtyard has been fitted with a mirror, which obscures the garden's real boundaries. The mirror also amplifies the light level, as do the white walls. The design is cool and formal, with a palette of green, white, and silver. A life-sized lead lion overlooks the seating area that features white iron furniture and topiary junipers.

The Garden of Ms. Alexandra Marshall and Mr. James Carroll
WEST CEDAR STREET

Here, a basic L-shaped plot has been given rhythm and a sense of movement with the creative use of curves. A narrow brick walkway meanders between raised serpentine beds, and stone fruit baskets are posted at either side of the curved steps leading to the kitchen door. A curtain of ivy covers most of the boundary wall, providing a textured backdrop for rhododendron and holly, while clematis, hydrangea, and two Concord grapevines climb the wall of the kitchen wing. The time is early spring, and tulips bloom in beds that are just coming to life. In summer they will be filled with well-established perennials — ferns, hostas, campanulas, bleeding hearts — and patches of flowering annuals.

Flowers

The Garden of Mr. and Mrs. Donald J. M. Wilson
MOUNT VERNON STREET

About twenty-five years ago the owners of this house designed and constructed a huge crescent-shaped bed — a bold architectural feature that dramatically changed their featureless brick courtyard and created a separate level just for plants. This basic plan remains, though the plantings are forever changing because the gardener likes to experiment. She is also an accomplished flower arranger and it is rare to find a Beacon Hill garden with such a profusion of blooms. In this view pink dogwoods crown the gentle pastels of the New England spring. In the foreground are hostas, wild geraniums, Solomon's seal, and violets along with tulips, a dwarf boxwood, and a few young annuals. There is much variegated and light-green foliage, and many splashes of flower color. Pots are everywhere — grouped on the ground, hanging on the walls and from the balcony, and propped on window sills and ledges.

SHADE

The Garden of Mr. and Mrs. Henry Lee
MOUNT VERNON STREET

Cool and inviting, this well-established courtyard presents a peaceful tableau in tones of green — a clear demonstration that shade can be beautiful and that shade gardening provides its own rewards. The high brick walls create a sheltered setting for plants that enjoy living in the shadows: hosta, pachysandra, European ginger, and holly along with plenty of ivy and textural accents from potted annuals and various house plants. The garden is spanned by two trees, a paperbark maple and a fifty-year-old linden, which on sunny days throw patterns of dappled sunlight upon the garden floor, creating a sense of texture and softening the rectangular outlines of the walls. Near the sitting area is a three-tiered recirculating fountain punctuated by a small round pot overflowing with impatiens.

Two classic Beacon Hill gardens — simple, quiet, and green

The Garden of Mr. and Mrs. John D. Curtin, Jr.
CHESTNUT STREET

Dappled sunlight falls gently on this tranquil garden, which is divided in two parts. An open bricked area is used for parking. It is spanned by a pergola that supports a rampant (and productive) grapevine, which forms a shady green umbrella against the summer sun, then loses its leaves to admit winter light. Pictured here is the sitting-out area close to the house. Paved with bluestone, it is edged with ivy-filled beds. A small Japanese maple in a planter adds a lacy green accent. The Kousa dogwood is in bloom, and wisteria and hydrangea intertwine on the back wall of the house. Along the ivy-clad side walls are unusual wood panels with a Moorish motif.

The Garden of Dr. and Mrs. Theodore Ongaro
PINCKNEY STREET

The appeal of this leafy retreat lies in its utter simplicity. Every feature is comfortably scaled to the size of the courtyard. The slightly raised beds that hug the walls feature plants that are known to do well on Beacon Hill: ferns and hostas, rhododendron and holly, climbing hydrangea, a Kousa dogwood. A framed mirror is neatly centered on the wood fence; its diamond pattern echoes that of the trellis panels above. All combine to create a pleasant, shady spot, a sheltered outdoor room in which to eat or relax. To the left of the garden gate is an unusual small tree, a Harry Lauder's Walking Stick. With a dusting of snow it becomes a striking winter feature.

Specimens

The Garden of Dr. Lynda Schubert Bodman
CHESTNUT STREET

The sloping site of this basically formal garden has been terraced in four levels. Its most remarkable feature is a row of seven paper birch trees. Their stately white stalks provide dramatic vertical accents at ground level while their foliage is light and airy overhead. These trees grow wild in New England, but here in the city they are pampered like specimens. They are underplanted with several other species that are indigenous to our woodlands: mountain laurel, false Solomon's seal, and trillium. The herringbone-paved terraces are clean and uncluttered. The centerpiece of the largest terrace is a Moorish-style pool topped with a wrought-iron grate; early photographs show that the pool was in place before 1930.

HARMONY

The Garden of Mr. and Mrs. Marvin A. Collier
LIME STREET

This exquisite little garden came into being in 1970, when the owners filled
in a sunken courtyard to the first-floor level of the house. In the Japanese
tradition, the new garden was planned for viewing from inside, where
sliding glass doors in the dining room create a long glass wall. Therefore, the
garden needs to look attractive all year round. Except for four hawthorn
trees, the principal features are architectural: rectangular bluestone paving
and a slatted wood fence painted a soft, warm gray to harmonize with the
stone. The plantings are changed with the seasons; the winter scheme is
quite simple, with cut trees and greens arranged to look especially nice with
a dressing of snow. Here the courtyard is planted up for a special occasion in
early summer. It is a stunning composition in blue, white, and silver with
each plant carefully chosen, creating a scene of perfect harmony.

Two gardens yielding to the realities of urban life by providing space for the family car

The Garden of Mr. and Mrs. Thomas M. Claflin II
MOUNT VERNON STREET

This modest-sized, casual-looking courtyard plays several roles, both practical and pleasurable. While its wide serpentine beds contain a healthy green garden, the central bricked surface accommodates an automobile. A sheltered lower terrace serves as a summer breakfast area, and the sunnier corners are crowded with pots of flowering annuals and house plants, as well as herbs for the kitchen. The shady borders are dense and green with massed plantings of rhododendrons and azaleas along with holly, euonymus, and yews. A wisteria and several honeysuckles climb the tall wooden fence. This garden is loved and lived in; its overall effect is congenial and charming.

The Garden of Mr. and Mrs. Richmond Mayo-Smith
MOUNT VERNON STREET

With its focus on shape and texture, this small courtyard reflects the owners' interest in Japanese garden design. Japanese features appear everywhere: the loosely graveled parking area with "island" outcroppings of stone, the gnarled stems of hydrangea and wisteria, the scroll ends of the bamboo-shaded pergola, and two sculpted rock pools that combine the classic garden elements of stone and water. The plantings are also in keeping with the garden's oriental mood: two dwarf Japanese maple trees, miniature lilac and forsythia, and a weeping cherry. An espaliered yew and an ivy-clad ailanthus tree provide vertical features against the brick boundary wall.

FURNISHINGS

The Garden of Dr. and Mrs. Donald R. Korb
BRIMMER STREET

The sitting area in this long and narrow garden is positioned away from the house, where it catches some midday sun. One of its most striking features is the owners' collection of antique garden furniture, which is perfectly in keeping with the Victorian-era house. Painted white, the pieces are crisply silhouetted against both red brick and green foliage, and their distinctive style makes them the centerpiece of the garden. A stone path curves through a "woodland" area where massed astilbe and hostas grow in broken shade. Beneath a wide-branching hemlock and set against a hanging basket of fresh green ferns is the beguiling figure of a small girl holding a wildflower bouquet. A tall wood fence provides a handsome background for the evergreen foliage of laurel and rhododendron.

The Garden of Mrs. John Sullivan
CHESTNUT STREET

In just a few short years, this irregularly shaped little courtyard has become the quintessential Beacon Hill garden. Its transformation has been guided by its owner, an interior designer, who approached the task with a sure sense of style as well as access to wonderful accessories. She is also a gardener, and the plants are notable for their variety, their profusion, and their vigorous good health. In this scene from early summer, honeysuckle blooms above white miniature roses, while variegated hostas and ivy fill a bed beneath an eighteenth-century white stone Buddha head. There are antique urns in iron, stone, and marble. The English ivy is not allowed to grow rampant; rather it is trained to grow decoratively over arches and along doorsteps. The false Federal-style doorway is a modest urban folly, installed by designer/architect Henry Sleeper in 1925.

NOSTALGIA

The Garden of Mrs. Earl H. Eacker
WEST CEDAR STREET

Some forty years old, this garden has acquired the impressive fullness that comes with maturity. Masonry, plants, accessories — all have aged gracefully to create a stunning ensemble with a strong sense of nostalgia. The garden's focal point is the lead figure of a shepherdess holding a young lamb, cast from an eighteenth-century English model. The statue is poised above a small reflecting pool flanked by low plantings of ferns and ginger. To the right of the pool is a white-blooming rhododendron, balanced on the left by a large mountain laurel, which comes into bloom just as the rhododendron fades. The back wall is clad with a vigorous climbing hydrangea. The herringbone brickwork adds additional richness and texture — an effect that has been likened to a Persian carpet. The total effect is cool, green, and timeless.

PATINA

The Garden of Mr. and Mrs. Richard A. Gargiulo
WEST CEDAR STREET

When they moved into their house in 1980, the present owners took an abandoned side yard and added some significant architectural features. At the far end of the yard they created a large raised terrace, five feet deep and raised some thirty inches toward the open sky. This was filled with a collection of shade-loving plants, which have now attained full maturity. The concave wall of the terrace inscribes one side of a great brick circle, which swells across the pavement at the rear of the garden to give the illusion of extra width. The circle motif is echoed in an ornamental bronze sundial in the form of an armillary sphere. Raised on a plinth, it makes a handsome garden centerpiece. The whitewashed side walls are heavily clad with English ivy, and the evergreen plantings have grown tall and full. The entire garden has acquired a rich patina, presenting a scene of year-round greenery as viewed from the house.

ANTIQUES

The Garden of Mr. and Mrs. Walter W. Patten, Jr.
WEST CEDAR STREET

This miniature formal landscape began to take shape some thirty years ago, when the owners developed a vision of a traditional box parterre as seen from their dining room windows. While the design has continued to evolve, it has always relied on closely trimmed boxwood and English ivy — and the owners' growing collection of garden antiques. Near the back wall is a small wrought-iron Regency settee, circa 1800, and a late-eighteenth-century carved urn attributed to Samuel McIntyre of Salem. English Coade stone figures representing the Four Seasons are placed within the greenery along with topiary boxwoods in containers. The rear wall is constructed of tightly-spaced *treillage* stained a dark green, and a custom-designed circular staircase climbs to a roofdeck terrace. An eighteenth-century French copper watering can — a rare survivor — guards the staircase. The two trees are a silver bell and a Kousa dogwood.

Whimsy

The Garden of Mr. and Mrs. Nicholas Negroponte
MOUNT VERNON STREET

This house has a large front yard where serious gardening is practiced. In the rear is a tight and sunless areaway, which was redesigned by the owners to provide an attractive view from a spare bedroom and which is "decorated" for arriving guests. Of necessity, the architectural effects are as important as the plantings. The prevailing spirit is one of good humor and whimsy: a salvaged wood pediment surmounts a "door" that is hung with an exquisite floral wreath; at the "doorstep" a potted tree peony is shaded by a pretty Japanese parasol. From stone containers grow kiwi vines that have survived several years in this sheltered spot. Wood planters contain columnar hollies, azaleas, and veronica, while clematis climbs the trompe l'oeil trellis above.

TRADITION
WALNUT STREET

Behind a Federal mansion on Walnut Street, there was once a large and beautiful garden, for many years a favorite on the club's annual spring tour. With changing times, however, the house proved too big for a single family, and when it was split into two condominiums in 1978 the garden was also divided. Happily the new owners have respected the tradition of the older garden, and it remains a visual unit.

The gardens are approached via a steep stairway of rough-hewn stone, which gives the lower courtyard a cloistered, old-world feeling.

The Garden of Mr. and Mrs. E. Denis Walsh

The smaller part of the original garden is long and narrow but also open and sunny. Here, near the fence dividing the two gardens, is an old-fashioned cutting garden — a bold endeavor on Beacon Hill but an obvious success. Tall plants at the back of the border include day lilies, coneflowers, phlox, and cosmos. Coreopsis and zinnias grow behind a neat edging of ageratum.

The Garden of Mr. and Mrs. Donald G. Paige

Framed by an arched iron gateway entwined with bittersweet (*left, below*) is a rare city view: a spacious lawn surrounded by trees and shrubbery. The planting scheme is simple with perimeter beds dense with pachysandra, providing a rich green setting for trees and shrubs and statuary. The garden's centerpiece is a fountain animated with a jet of bright water. Surrounded by various annuals and perennials, it is also a summer splashing pool for children.

SCULPTURE

The Garden of Mr. and Mrs. Thomas M. Clyde
CHESTNUT STREET

Nestled deep in the hillside, this is a sunken garden, green and serene. The narrow side beds contain a healthy ground cover of English ivy, whose glossy dark foliage is allowed to climb the whitewashed stone foundations on the end wall. Tall, tightly spaced latticework provides privacy but admits a lovely, shimmering light from the sunny garden beyond. The extreme height of the wall is broken by a small iron balcony whose design incorporates several antique cast-iron medallions. The finishing touch is a recent arrival, a nineteenth-century figure of a goddess or maiden holding a scallop shell. She stands in a protected area beneath the balcony. With a beautifully weathered surface, the sculpture is perfectly suited to the site and punctuates the garden with a stunning, romantic focal point.

INDIVIDUALITY

The Garden of Mr. and Mrs. Maurice E. Frye, Jr.
REVERE STREET

Quite unlike any other space on Beacon Hill, this courtyard is partially
sheltered by a long, low roof, which creates a protected alcove that the
family uses as an extension of their house. It is fully furnished, with a dining
table and chairs and a living area with vintage wicker pieces, painted black.
This is in every sense an outdoor room. Beyond is a very shady garden
where several varieties of hosta have taken hold along with ferns and
woodland wildflowers accented by the blossoms of impatiens and begonias.
Other plants are mostly in containers. At the rear of the garden is a small
potting shed and a gate leading to an ancient pedestrian passage known as
Pump Lane. Throughout the courtyard are pieces of sculpture, architectural
ornaments, and other personal touches that give this garden its
individualized character and style.

VERSATILITY

The Garden of Mr. and Mrs. William B. O'Keeffe
CHESTNUT STREET

The basic plan of this garden was formal and symmetrical. Earlier plantings by the present owners had always aimed to soften this look with informal evergreen material, but the results were never satisfactory. Inspiration came with a visit to the boxwood gardens of Charleston, South Carolina, where the owner began to see her own garden in a new light. The idea developed of a more versatile planting scheme with "a neat box hedge all around, and moveable planters where I can experiment with foliage and flower combinations." Young boxwoods now surround the garden, with vertical accents from small upright yews and plumes of ornamental grass. Large terracotta containers are presently filled with ferns and tropical plants. One of the garden's most distinctive features is its paving, a strong pattern of stone rectangles interlaid with rows of old Beacon Hill bricks.

Sophistication

The Garden of Mr. and Mrs. Garret Schenck
LOUISBURG SQUARE

The steep and rugged character of the Hill's western slope is still evident in the terracing of this shady courtyard. The garden is also defined by its towering brick walls, which rise some fifty feet to create a setting of complete privacy. Inheriting these two features, the present owners have transformed a rather difficult space into a cool and sophisticated city garden. The walls have been painted a silvery gray as a background for greenery — and indeed, there is no color here except for shades of green and white. Lining the stairs and boundary walls are containers filled with white-flowering plants and boxwood topiaries. This is another garden owned by a professional designer, who has guided its plan and added her own outstanding collection of garden accessories — Italian terracotta statues, antique American urns, and vintage high-quality cast-iron furniture. Formal but not austere, this garden exemplifies urbanity and good taste.

The Garden of Mrs. Virginia M. Lawrence
PINCKNEY STREET

The oversized ornament has been on this wall for decades, but the rest of the garden is brand new. The space behind the house is shared with an automobile, so the actual garden area is only 12 by 20 feet. The design is strong and architectural, its oval plan contrasting with its rectangular boundaries; a sweeping arc interlocks with the three brick steps leading into the house. A wide variety of perennials and climbing vines, including clematis, honeysuckle, and porcelain berry, takes advantage of the different miniclimates of sun and shade that occur here. The small wall fountain is pleasing to the ear as well as the eye and masks the noises of the city.

The Garden of Mr. and Mrs. Dennis Keefe
MOUNT VERNON STREET

The prominent white plaque mounted between two brick piers gives this young garden a firm and formal focal point. Reproducing a fragment of the frieze of the Parthenon, it is in fact made of fiberglass. Beneath the plaque is a stone bench on scrolled bases, which continues the classical theme and establishes the basic symmetry of the garden's design. From either wall a low planting bed thrusts into the sunny center of the courtyard. The one on the right contains a threadleaf cypress and a Japanese maple, backed by a thick mantle of English ivy — the single feature of the earlier yard that the owners retained. In the foreground are white shrub roses and mountain laurel.

PERSISTENCE

The Garden of Susan McWhinney-Morse and David H. Morse
TEMPLE STREET

This leafy green tunnel is truly a triumph. Under the most adverse conditions, its owner has labored for many years, persisting through a succession of failures until finally achieving a living, growing garden. At base was a severe problem with light — no sunlight ever touches any part of this courtyard, which is a long, thin corridor traversed by a narrow brick path. Today the walkway is edged with a verdant border, while high wood boxes overflow with healthy plants. The star performers in this garden are the hostas. Six varieties grow here, among them the huge, golden edged "Francis Williams." The prevailing rich green is broken by light-colored foliage and occasional flecks of color. Despite extremely limited natural light, the plants themselves seem to put forth a shimmering glow, and the overall effect is somewhat magical.

SERENDIPITY

The Garden of Mrs. John M. Kingsland
PINCKNEY STREET

The brick path that passes the doorway of this house is a section of a former
public right-of-way that dates from the eighteenth century, when much of
the neighborhood consisted of small frame houses like this one. It provides a
picturesque site for one of the smallest and most engaging of the Hidden
Gardens. The footpath is now privately owned and the house itself hidden
from the street. A narrow garden has been tucked alongside a tall
neighboring building. While shady, it has full sun at midday and the most
successful plants are woodland species: pulmonaria, ginger, hosta, ferns, and
goatsbeard. There are two hemlock trees, an azalea, and a dwarf Japanese
maple. The garden's newest feature is a naturalistic fountain fashioned from
native rocks, from which water trickles gently into a tiny pool containing a
miniature water garden.

CLIMBERS

The Garden of Lise and Myles Striar
PINCKNEY STREET

Since the sober outlines of this formal garden were drawn some forty years ago, its symmetrical design has been softened by an exuberance of climbing plants. Today the boundary walls are covered with six different mature climbers: wisteria, hydrangea, clematis, English ivy, China fleece vine, and Dutchman's pipe — each given a severe annual pruning then left to grow its own free way. The floor is paved with multicolored rectangular flagstones near the house and glazed red brick on the upper terrace. The change of level is also defined by a handsome wrought-iron fence and gate, with flanking brick piers that support iron urns containing geraniums and petunias. Here and throughout the garden there is an unusually high quality in both materials and workmanship that dates from the original design — which, aging most gracefully, has stood the test of time.

The Garden of Mrs. George Herrmann
PINCKNEY STREET

Paved in brick and multicolored slate, this is a semi-wild woodland garden
where massed and mixed foliage creates a rich tapestry of green on green.
The planting is dense and natural looking, with the fresh green fronds of
ferns and stately plumes of flowering goatsbeard along with glossy dark holly
and silver-edged hostas. House plants, too, enjoy the sheltered setting, and
they spend the entire summer in its shady borders, returning indoors each
fall refreshed and renewed. The oval stone table on the lower terrace has
been fashioned from an old cistern cover, excavated from this yard when the
garden was being built.

The Garden of Dr. and Mrs. J. Wallace McMeel
WEST CEDAR STREET

A mere six feet wide, this is the long arm of an L-shaped courtyard — a
most difficult site. But through trial and error its owners have created a
garden that is not only pleasing to the eye but horticulturally interesting.
The long raised bed is packed with plants, which spill over the low
bluestone wall to soften the edge of the pathway. Height is provided by a
pair of viburnums and a weeping white birch, an unusual tree, especially in
the city. The thick green underplanting is composed of the simplest of
plants, thoughtfully chosen — violets, ginger, a variety of hostas — which
weave together to form a rich pastiche of textured foliage.

TERRACING

The Garden of Mr. and Mrs. Wat H. Tyler
PINCKNEY STREET

The owners, who designed the garden themselves, knew exactly what they wanted: an evergreen view from the windows of their business office on the ground floor of the house. The plan they adopted was a scaled-down version of a design they had seen for a larger garden, with four tiers of curved terraces connected by broad stone steps. It was a complex scheme, involving months of excavation and construction, but the results are stunning. The terraces are neatly built of reclaimed brick with bluestone coping, and they have been densely planted. The lower tiers, nearest the house, receive the least light, so they hold woodland evergreens. The sunnier upper levels are filled with various free-blooming annuals along with lilacs, peonies, and roses. The terraces have created extra space for planting as well as extra seating for a crowd. The small basin fed from a lion mask makes an artful focal point.

The Garden of Mr. and Mrs. John D. Spooner
CHESTNUT STREET

Carved deep into the hillside, this courtyard proved too shady to support any permanent plantings. After countless failures the owners abandoned dirt gardening in favor of a different approach. Except for a pair of young wisteria vines and a small amount of ivy, everything is in containers, which can be replanted and rearranged seasonally. In this springtime view, some are ablaze with yellow tulips while others still slumber beneath winter blankets of moss. Like the containers, the paving displays a variety of shapes, colors, and textures. The garden's key feature is an eighteenth-century terracotta figure of a monk, said to have come from an Italian monastery via Newport. Black trompe l'oeil trelliswork adds interest to the garden's back wall.

The Garden of Mr. and Mrs. Albert H. Elfner
CHESTNUT STREET

A mere 15 by 20 feet and shadowed by high walls, this tiny courtyard is almost entirely paved with brick. In its one sunny corner a bleeding heart and a hosta grow in a patch of open ground. Everything else is in pots. The stuccoed side wall is painted a creamy white, reflecting a warm light that brightens the whole garden. There are clusters of potted plants and many decorative touches: a nineteenth-century glazed Chinese garden stool, Quimper wall planters, a mirror in a filigree frame, and a lead wall fountain flanked by urns containing fifteen-year-old spathiphyllums. This creative use of accessories has transformed a dark and featureless cul-de-sac into a pretty summer sitting room.

PROFUSION

The Garden of Mr. and Mrs. Robert L. Fondren
JOY STREET

Not many Beacon Hill yards will support a rose bed, but here on Joy Street is proof it can be done. Planned to reach its peak in high summer, the garden contains three varieties of roses, along with a profusion of free-blooming plants that recalls an English cottage garden. The raised beds are retained by timbers; they contain a selection of annuals along with bleeding hearts, white campanulas, astilbe, and a tree peony. This seasonal show of color is set against a thick backdrop of climbers, which screens the garden on all sides and nearly obscures its boundaries. Here and there trellis panels have been added for extra privacy. Along the rear wall a climbing hydrangea creates a lacy pattern, its great round flower heads highlighted with bright pinpoints of white. Nearby is an artful arrangement of containers, some of them raised on chimney pots.

REMEMBRANCES

The Garden of Mr. and Mrs. James McNeely
WEST CEDAR STREET

Each spring this garden is dominated by the pink blossoms of a large and spreading crabapple tree, but in midsummer the color scheme changes as the trumpet vine comes into vibrant flower. This vigorous plant was grown from a cutting taken some thirty years ago from the owner's childhood home in Pennsylvania, and only harsh pruning keeps it in bounds. Scattered in the borders are additional remembrances of family and friends; the coral bells, the violets, and the hellebores all arrived here as mementos of a particular time and place. This garden has long been the scene of experimental plantings and its borders support a lively collection of plants, some of them unusual in the city. The narrow bed on the left is packed with perennials: a tree peony, amsonia, bleeding hearts, Dutchman's britches, and Siberian iris, along with violets, grape hyacinths, and other early bulbs. The young tree in the far corner is a Franklinia, newly planted to replace a fine old dogwood that was lost in a winter storm.

SECLUSION

The Garden of Mr. and Mrs. Lawrence Coolidge
MOUNT VERNON STREET

Seen here on a misty summer morning, this is the only Hidden Garden
without walls. Rather, it is screened by a dense planting of trees and shrubs,
creating a secluded family sitting area that is invisible from the nearby street.
The garden is entered via a flagstone pathway from the house, an 1802 brick
mansion designed by Charles Bulfinch. The stone patio is surrounded on
three sides by shrubbery — azaleas and andromeda backed by taller lilacs,
forsythia, and rhododendrons. Edging the flagstones are perennial plantings
of ginger and barren strawberry with accents from white and pink
impatiens. A pair of antique urns echoes the classical spirit of the house;
they are planted with bright red geraniums and trailing ivy.

THE ANNIE FIELDS GARDEN

With its broad lawn and towering old trees, the Annie Fields Garden presents a surprising landscape for Beacon Hill, and indeed this is a rare place. It retains the name of its first owner, Annie Adams Fields, who maintained a garden on this site from the time of her marriage in 1854 until her death six decades later. James T. Fields was a prominent publisher and his home was a meeting place for the literary lions of the day — from local luminaries like Hawthorne, Emerson, and Whittier to visiting celebrities like Thackeray and Dickens. Annie Fields' diaries chronicle these many friendships alongside a lively account of her day-by-day affairs, including time working in her beloved garden. We know, for example, that apple trees and grapevines grew here with lilac and wisteria, crocuses and violets.

The Fields' Charles Street house is long since demolished and the wide bay it overlooked is now a mere river, but the garden survives, the proud possession of the fourteen households that today surround it.

At first glance the thick green border appears to be a single unit, while in fact it is portioned among the abutting homeowners, each owning several yards of planting bed. The garden is communally maintained.

The Garden of Mr. and Mrs. Edward C. Johnson 3d
CHARLES RIVER SQUARE

Annie Fields makes specific mention of linden trees, and one one-hundred-year-old European linden still grows here. In its shade is a simple massed planting of lily of the valley — an old-fashioned flower most appropriate to this place.

The Garden of Dr. and Mrs. Desmond H. Birkett
CHARLES RIVER SQUARE

This strip of border is typical of the plantings that surround the Annie Fields Garden, with hosta, violets, and a variegated barberry; peonies and day lilies give seasonal color.

FLAIR

The Garden of Mr. and Mrs. Robert T. O'Connell
LOUISBURG SQUARE

This long, thin strip of land drops down the hillside in a series of small terraces. It has been imaginatively redesigned by its new owner, who has divided the space into several compartments and treated each one individually. The garden begins just outside the kitchen door with a lighthearted folly — a small square outdoor room fitted with a Federal-style marble mantelpiece, candelabra sconces, and a pair of facing settees. Several short flights of steps lead to the lower garden, which is larger and more open. Here a brick terrace is surrounded by abundant greenery, with a stunning row of matched pyramidal hollies and low boxwood hedges enclosing massed plantings of lilies and hydrangeas. Mounted high on the wall is a bull's eye window, an architectural remnant from a French mansard roof, that has been fitted with a mirror. On every level this attractive new garden displays creativity and flair.

DRAMA

The Garden of Mr. and Mrs. William A. Sherden
WALNUT STREET

With its rugged terrain and some beautiful old stonework, this hillside site conjures up a sense of mystery and drama. The owners took advantage of these qualities to create a garden that is quite unlike the Hill's typical red-brick courtyards. Two wedge-shaped steps rise steeply to the upper terrace, from which a stepping-stone path climbs to a secluded garden bench set against a towering wood fence that is painted a rich, deep blue. Sheltered by an enormous ash tree, it commands a view back down the slope, which is planted with simple woodland evergreens. Brick and stonework are combined harmoniously, but the prevailing material is stone — particularly the massive retaining wall, which probably dates from the earliest years of permanent settlement on Beacon Hill.

*Two older gardens adapting to an altered environment and to the changing
requirements of a growing family*

The Garden of Mr. and Mrs. Daniel Taylor
PHILLIPS STREET

Unusally open and airy, this North Slope garden occupies the back yards of
two nineteenth-century tenements. Much earlier it was the site of two small
frame houses, now disappeared,1 that fronted a pedestrian lane. Today's
garden was gradually developed by the owners during the 1970s, beginning
as a children's play yard and slowly evolving into this pleasant outdoor
family room. Near the back fence is a dogwood and an ailanthus, while
several mock oranges rise from the shady bed on the left. Two hundred
white impatiens are planted here each year. Tucked into planting beds,
hanging baskets, and various containers, their crisp bright blossoms sparkle
from even the darkest corner.

The Garden of Mr. and Mrs. Thomas E. Weesner
PINCKNEY STREET

Over a period of twenty-five years the microclimate in this south-facing yard
has changed several times — from deeply shaded to sunny and bright with
the removal of a large elm in the 1970s, and then a gradual return to shady
conditions as replacement trees have matured. Today it is roofed over by the
canopies of three trees — a woodland setting. The mounded bed on the
right occupies the site of the old elm. It holds perennial shade lovers: ferns,
miniature astilbes and hostas, lamiums, brunnera, May apples, pulmonaria.
Sharing the sunny bed on the left is a Kousa dogwood and a traditional
Beacon Hill lamp post along with cotoneaster and spring-flowering deutzia.

SCALE

The Garden of Mr. and Mrs. Michael K. Tooke
MOUNT VERNON STREET

The challenge in designing this unusually large garden was the shape of the plot — very long and relatively narrow with high walls that made it seem even narrower. The solution has been to divide the site in half, with two separate enclosures, each of a more pleasing scale. Here is a view looking into the more formal part of the garden, where the central pathway fans out into a large paved circle — a granite centerpiece surrounded by bricks in a radiating pattern. This feature provides a focal point midway to the house, relieving the corridor effect but still allowing plenty of space for plants. This part of the garden has three courtyard-sized understory trees, a Stewartia and two Kousa dogwoods, along with beds of evergreens and a sprinkling of flowering annuals. Below the climbing red roses next to the kitchen wing is a stone cherub perched in a shell birdbath, sculpted by a relative of one of the owners.

The Garden of Sandra and Richard W. Ilgen
West Cedar Street

Here is a dooryard garden with a cottage-style charm, designed by its owners eight years ago to be enjoyed from the windows of their new sunroom. The gardener in the family has been experimenting with plants for many years, and her expertise is evident in every corner of this tiny plot. Measuring only about 12 by 15 feet, it is skillfully planned to allow as much space as possible for plants. Rectangular slate pavers cut a diagonal path across the courtyard, which is shaded by two spring-flowering trees, a shad in the foreground and a tree lilac near the house. The planting is busy and varied, with dozens of well-tended specimens thoughtfully located according to their growing requirements. Beneath the shad tree is a shade garden, sheltered by a hedge of shapely boxwoods. Perennials grow near the lilac, while herbs and potted plants are grouped beside the sunroom door. In the shade garden are an engaging stone putto and an old-fashioned gazing ball.

FINESSE

The Garden of Mr. and Mrs. Samuel Robert
MOUNT VERNON STREET

A horseshoe staircase descends grandly from the house into this fine garden with its modest-sized lawn encircled by a brick pathway. The Victorian-era house was erected on a more imposing scale than any of its neighbors, and its garden, too, is unusually large. It is designed with a fine finesse, from the graceful double stairway to the classical little "tool temple" in the far corner of the yard. To the left of the stairs are rhododendron and leucothoe, balanced on the opposite side by a bed of double pink roses. Beneath the balcony is a dense bamboo thicket. Hydrangeas bloom brightly in containers. Decorative items include the antique Moroccan bird cage hanging from the balcony and an armillary sphere mounted on an old cast-stone baluster. A large street tree overhanging the garden wall provides a welcome sense of seclusion along with extra greenery.

CREATIVITY

The Garden of Ms. Deborah R. Hanley and Mr. Francis D. McGuire
PINCKNEY STREET

Every corner of this courtyard reflects the creativity of its owners, who in eighteen years have turned a featureless service area into the engaging little garden seen here. The architectural bones of the garden are its massive raised beds, which form a distinct second level devoted entirely to plants. Constructed of native fieldstone, they provide a natural setting for climbing and trailing ivy along with a rich collection of mostly evergreen plants. A sunny patch along the back wall supports roses, spirea, and a white-blooming lilac, while an arborvitae gives a prominent vertical accent beside the garden gate. In this late September scene, the garden strikes a harvest theme with seasonal arrangements of pumpkins, gourds, and Indian corn. Autumn Joy sedum and a massed planting of white chrysanthemums will provide interest through the long New England fall.

TRELLIS

The Garden of Mr. and Mrs. William F. Yates
CHESTNUT STREET

Trelliswork contributes a lot to this young garden, which was installed in
1993. It heightens the rear wall for privacy, and until the plantings mature it
adds texture and interest to all the walls while providing a foothold for a
collection of young climbers. Ivy, clematis, honeysuckle, and roses will
eventually clothe much of the trellis, but meanwhile the open squares of
lattice, painted a gleaming white and topped with finials, brighten the
garden and give it a formal touch. The planting scheme, however, is basically
informal, with relaxed, textured beds of mixed perennials and annuals. The
dwarf blue spruce anchoring the corner has already become an architectural
feature as a vertical accent. Three other trees are tucked into this relatively
small space — two Kousa dogwoods and a Japanese maple, along with five
hardy hibiscus standards.

Annually, on the third Thursday of May, the Hidden Gardens Tour attracts thousands of visitors. Proceeds from that event and revenues from the sale of this book give direct financial support to dozens of local, state, and national programs and also fund the club's own civic planting projects. Shown clockwise from left are views from four of these undertakings: the Memorial Garden at Old North Church; plantings at the West End Branch of the Boston Public Library; Codman Island at the corner of Beacon and Charles streets; and the garden at Peter Faneuil House on South Russell Street.